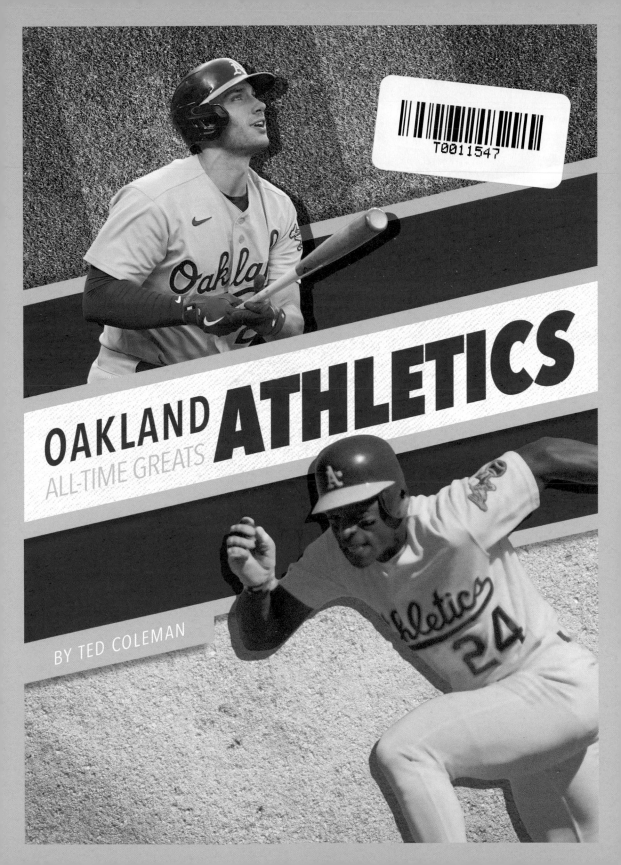

OAKLAND ATHLETICS
ALL-TIME GREATS

BY TED COLEMAN

T0011547

Book design by Jake Slavik
Cover design by Jake Slavik

Photographs ©: Ted S. Warren/AP Images, cover (top), 1 (top); NewsBase/AP Images, cover (bottom), 1 (bottom); AP Images, 4, 6, 8, 14; Icon Sportswire/AP Images, 10; Al Messerschmidt/AP Images, 12; Bob Galbraith/AP Images, 16; Eric Risberg/AP Images, 18; Jeff Chiu/AP Images, 20

Press Box Books, an imprint of Press Room Editions.

ISBN
978-1-63494-506-6 (library bound)
978-1-63494-532-5 (paperback)
978-1-63494-582-0 (epub)
978-1-63494-558-5 (hosted ebook)

Library of Congress Control Number: 2022901753

Distributed by North Star Editions, Inc.
2297 Waters Drive
Mendota Heights, MN 55120
www.northstareditions.com

Printed in the United States of America
082022

ABOUT THE AUTHOR

Ted Coleman is a freelance sportswriter and children's book author who lives in Louisville, Kentucky, with his trusty Affenpinscher, Chloe.

TABLE OF CONTENTS

PLANK

CHAPTER 1
CONNIE MACK'S ATHLETICS

The Oakland Athletics started out in 1901. Back then, they played in Philadelphia, Pennsylvania. The A's were one of the best teams in the American League (AL). Legendary manager Connie Mack led them to three World Series titles by 1913. Star pitcher **Eddie Plank** spent 14 seasons with the team. He won at least 20 games in seven of those seasons.

STAT SPOTLIGHT

CAREER WINS
ATHLETICS TEAM RECORD
Eddie Plank: 284

BENDER

Alongside Plank was right-hander **Charles Bender**. He was an American Indian of the Ojibwe Nation. Bender had to deal with racism on the field. But he was able to rise above it and dominate on the mound. From 1909 through 1914, Bender had a record of 109-39.

Behind the team's great pitchers were two of the best infielders in the game. Second baseman **Eddie Collins** could do just about everything on the field. In his 13 years with the A's, he racked up 1,308 hits, 373 stolen bases, and 85 triples.

At third base was **Frank "Home Run" Baker.** Players didn't hit many home runs in the 1910s. Even so, Baker led the AL in homers every year from 1911 to 1914.

CONNIE MACK

Connie Mack was there for the first 50 years of Athletics baseball. Mack wasn't just the team's manager. He was also the owner. Mack recorded 3,731 wins during his major league career. That's nearly 1,000 more than the manager in second place. Mack was known as a gentleman. Baseball managers usually wear the team's uniform during games. But Mack always wore a suit and tie.

FOXX
3

COCHRANE
2

SIMMONS
7

The early A's had great players. However, they often struggled to make money. Mack usually built a good team and then sold his stars to raise cash. As a result, the team didn't have much success in the late 1910s and early 1920s. But by 1929, Philadelphia was back on top. Led by first baseman **Jimmie Foxx**, the A's won the World Series that year. Foxx belted two home runs in the series.

Mickey Cochrane was another key member of the team. Cochrane was one of the greatest catchers in history. He won the Most Valuable Player (MVP) Award in 1928. But he was perhaps best known for his fiery temper.

Another star of that era was outfielder **Al Simmons**. His real last name was Szymanski. But he changed it to Simmons so it would be easier to pronounce. During his 12 years with the A's, Simmons had an incredible .356 batting average.

Pitcher **Robert "Lefty" Grove** didn't start playing baseball until he was 19. He took to the game quickly, though. Grove ended up winning 195 games for the A's. He also helped the team become champions once again. Grove won two games in the 1930 World Series.

HUNTER
27

CHAPTER 2
THE MUSTACHE GANG

In the 1950s, several baseball teams moved west. The Athletics were one of them. They moved to Kansas City in 1955. But after 13 straight losing seasons, the A's moved even further west. In 1968, they settled in Oakland, California.

By that point, the A's already had some young stars. One was pitcher **Jim "Catfish" Hunter**. The nickname was given to him by Charlie Finley, the team's new owner. Finley thought the silly nickname would bring in more fans. Hunter didn't like it. But he showed promise on the mound. He threw a perfect

JACKSON
9

game in 1968. Hunter won a total of 161 games for the A's. He also won the Cy Young Award in 1974.

Bert Campaneris was also with the A's when they moved from Kansas City. The speedy shortstop led the AL in stolen bases six times.

Reggie Jackson joined the Athletics in 1967. In his 10 seasons with the A's, Jackson made the All-Star team six times. The brash outfielder earned the nickname "Mr. October" for his clutch hitting in the postseason. He also won the MVP Award in 1973.

By 1972, Oakland was the best team in baseball. Leading the way was left fielder **Joe Rudi**. His leaping catch in Game 2 of the World Series was a key defensive play. It helped Oakland beat the Cincinnati Reds for the title.

CHARLIE O.

Charles Oscar Finley was one of baseball's strangest owners. He changed the team's colors from blue and white to green, gold, and white. He also had the players wear white shoes. But Finley had even wilder ideas. He wanted the league to change the balls from white to orange. He also adopted a live mule as the team's mascot. The mule, named Charlie-O, sometimes showed up at parties with Finley.

14

The A's of the 1970s built another dynasty. They won the World Series again in 1973 and 1974. In those two seasons, third baseman **Sal Bando** totaled 51 home runs and 201 runs batted in (RBI).

The A's also had great pitching. **Vida Blue** threw one of the hardest fastballs in the game. In 1971, he won both the MVP Award and the Cy Young Award. That season, Blue won 24 games and struck out 301 batters.

Perhaps the most recognizable player of that era was **Rollie Fingers**. Fingers was an excellent relief pitcher. He also sported a large, curly mustache. He grew it after Finley offered the players extra money to grow facial hair. Several other players joined Fingers. The Oakland A's of the 1970s became known as the "Mustache Gang."

ECKERSLEY
43

CHAPTER 3
THE MODERN A'S

After their success in the 1970s, the Athletics sank back down the standings for most of the next decade. But in 1988, they were back again. This time, the team was led by manager Tony La Russa. He helped the team reach three straight World Series. And in 1989, the A's won it all. They defeated the nearby San Francisco Giants in a four-game sweep.

Dennis Eckersley played a big role in the team's success. The relief pitcher recorded 320 saves in his nine years with Oakland. Relievers rarely win the MVP Award. But Eckersley did in

HENDERSON
24

1992. That season, he had 51 saves with a 1.91 earned run average (ERA).

The A's also had two great sluggers. **Jose Canseco** was one of the most feared hitters in baseball. In 1988, he led the AL with 42 home runs and 124 RBIs. It was no surprise that he won the MVP Award that year.

Mark McGwire was another powerful hitter. In 1987, he set an MLB rookie record with 49 home runs. McGwire and Canseco became known as the "Bash Brothers." Instead of high-fiving, they celebrated home runs by bumping their muscular forearms together.

The A's weren't all about power, though. The team also had plenty of speed. **Rickey Henderson** was the greatest base stealer the game has ever seen. In 1982 alone, he stole 130 bases. Henderson was also an outstanding leadoff hitter. He cranked out 167 home runs during his 14 seasons with Oakland.

STAT SPOTLIGHT

CAREER HOME RUNS
ATHLETICS TEAM RECORD
Mark McGwire: 363

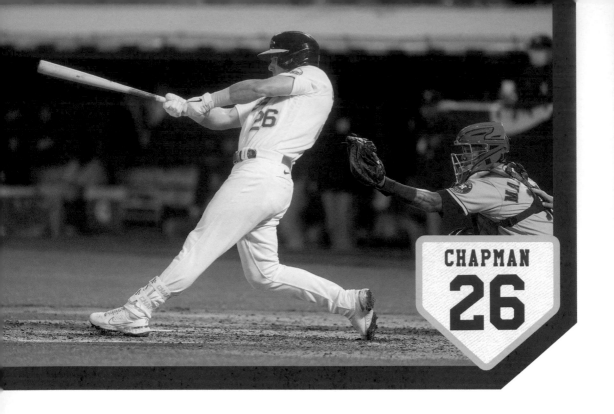

CHAPMAN
26

The A's enjoyed more success in the early 2000s. They reached the postseason five times from 2000 to 2006. Third baseman **Eric Chavez** was a consistent hitter. Four times during his career, he drove in more than 100 runs.

But the A's of the 2000s were mostly known for their pitching. **Tim Hudson**, **Mark Mulder**, and **Barry Zito** were three of baseball's best starters. Zito went 23–5 in 2002. He also won the Cy Young Award that year.

From 2018 through 2021, the A's had four winning seasons in a row. They also made the postseason three times. Power-hitting infielders **Matt Chapman** and **Matt Olson** led the way. Through 2021, Chapman recorded 111 home runs in 573 career games. Meanwhile, Olson had 142 homers in 575 games. A's fans hoped it wouldn't be long before the team celebrated another World Series title.

NUMBERS GAME

In the early 2000s, the Athletics didn't have as much money as most other teams. General manager Billy Beane knew Oakland couldn't afford star players with huge contracts. So, Beane focused on other ways to get good players. He used statistics. That helped him find less-expensive players who were better than other teams realized. The idea worked. Oakland ended up with great teams in the early 2000s.

TIMELINE

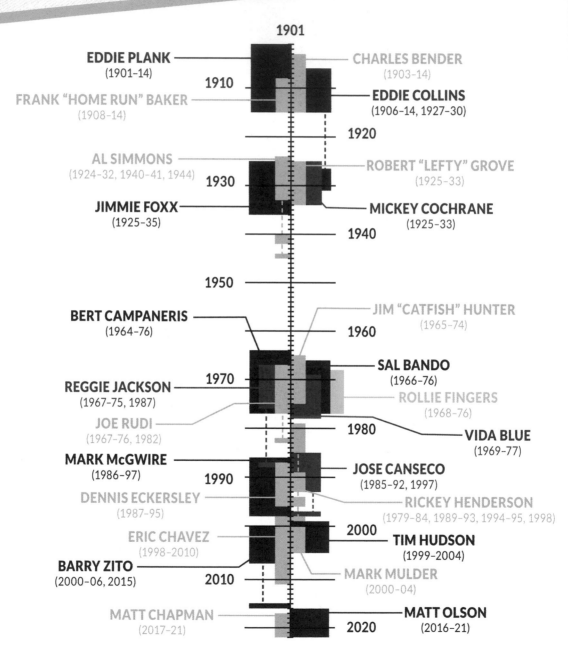

1901

EDDIE PLANK — (1901–14)

CHARLES BENDER (1903–14)

1910

FRANK "HOME RUN" BAKER — (1908–14)

EDDIE COLLINS — (1906–14, 1927–30)

1920

AL SIMMONS (1924–32, 1940–41, 1944)

ROBERT "LEFTY" GROVE (1925–33)

1930

JIMMIE FOXX (1925–35)

MICKEY COCHRANE (1925–33)

1940

1950

JIM "CATFISH" HUNTER (1965–74)

BERT CAMPANERIS (1964–76)

1960

SAL BANDO (1966–76)

REGGIE JACKSON (1967–75, 1987)

1970

ROLLIE FINGERS (1968–76)

JOE RUDI (1967–76, 1982)

1980

VIDA BLUE (1969–77)

MARK McGWIRE (1986–97)

1990

JOSE CANSECO (1985–92, 1997)

DENNIS ECKERSLEY (1987–95)

RICKEY HENDERSON (1979–84, 1989–93, 1994–95, 1998)

ERIC CHAVEZ (1998–2010)

2000

TIM HUDSON (1999–2004)

BARRY ZITO (2000–06, 2015)

2010

MARK MULDER (2000–04)

MATT CHAPMAN (2017–21)

2020

MATT OLSON (2016–21)

TEAM FACTS

OAKLAND ATHLETICS

Team history: Philadelphia Athletics (1901–54), Kansas City Athletics (1955–67), Oakland Athletics (1968–)

World Series titles: 9 (1910, 1911, 1913, 1929, 1930, 1972, 1973, 1974, 1989)*

Key managers:

Connie Mack (1901–50)

3,582–3,814 (.484), 5 World Series titles

Dick Williams (1971–73)

288–190 (.603), 2 World Series titles

Tony La Russa (1986–95)

798–673 (.542), 1 World Series title

MORE INFORMATION

To learn more about the Oakland Athletics, go to **pressboxbooks.com/AllAccess**.

These links are routinely monitored and updated to provide the most current information available.

*through 2021

GLOSSARY

clutch
Having to do with a difficult situation when the outcome of the game is in question.

dynasty
A team that has an extended period of success, usually winning multiple championships in the process.

era
A period of time in history.

leadoff
The first batter in a team's lineup.

perfect game
A game in which a pitcher doesn't allow any batters to reach base.

reliever
A pitcher who does not start the game.

rookie
A professional athlete in his or her first year of competition.

statistics
The use of numbers to find answers to specific questions.

INDEX